Books should be returned on or before the
last date stamped below

Pluto and the Search for New Planets

By Gregory Vogt

Raintree

OUR UNIVERSE

www.raintreepublishers.co.uk
Visit our website to find out more information about Raintree books.

To order:

📞 Phone 44 (0)1865 888112

📄 Send a fax to 44 (0)1865 314091

💻 Visit the Raintree Bookshop at www.raintreepublishers.co.uk to browse our catalogue and order online.

J523.482
1215719

First published in Great Britain by Raintree Publishers, Halley Court, Jordan Hill, Oxford OX2 8EJ, part of Harcourt Education.
Raintree is a registered trademark of Harcourt Education Ltd.

Design: Jo Hinton-Malivoire and Tinstar Design (www.tinstar.co.uk), Jo Sapwell (www.tipani.co.uk)
Illustrations: Art Construction
Picture Research: Maria Joannou and Su Alexander
Production: Jonathan Smith

Originated by Dot Gradation Ltd
Printed and bound in Hong Kong, China by South China Printing Co. Ltd.

ISBN 1 844 21416 8 (hardback)
06 05 04 03 02
10 9 8 7 6 5 4 3 2 1

British Library Cataloguing in Publication Data
Vogt, Gregory
Pluto and the search for new planets. - (Our universe)
1.Pluto (Planet) - Juvenile literature
I.Title
523.4'82

A full catalogue record for this book is available from the British Library.

Acknowledgements
The publishers would like to thank the following for permission to reproduce photographs:
Cover Photo; Dr. R. Albrecht, ESA/ESO Space Telescope European Coordinating Facility and NASA, title page; NASA, 6, 14, 16, 20, 22, 24, 28, 30, 32, 39; Solar & Heliospheric Observatory (SOHO), 10. SOHO is a project of international cooperation between ESA and NASA. Erich Karkoschka (University of Arizona) and NASA, 12; Bettmann/ CORBIS, 18; A. Stern (SwRI), M. Buie (Lowell Obs.), NASA, ESA, 26; C. Grady (NOAO at NASA Goddard Space Flight Center) and NASA, 40; Hubble Heritage Team (AURA/STScI/NASA), 44

Content Consultant
David Jewitt
Professor of Astronomy
University of Hawaii Institute for Astronomy

Contents

Any words appearing in the text in bold, **like this**, are explained in the glossary.

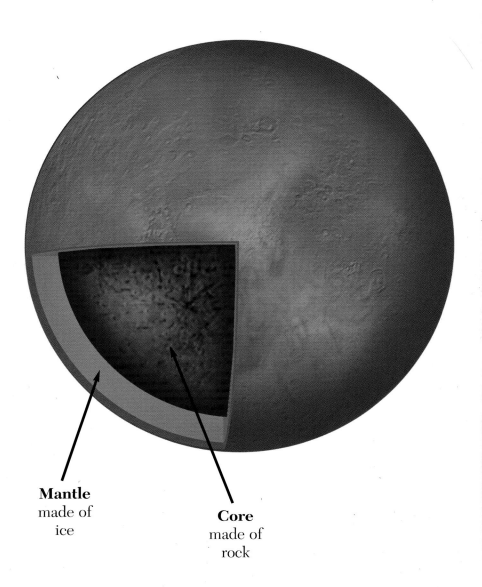

Mantle
made of
ice

Core
made of
rock

A quick look at Pluto

What is Pluto?
Pluto is the ninth planet in our solar system. At most points in its orbit, it is the furthest planet from the Sun.

What is Pluto made of?
Pluto is the only planet that is made mainly of rock and ice.

How big is Pluto?
Pluto is the smallest known planet in our solar system. It is about 2300 kilometres (1400 miles) in diameter. Diameter is the distance from one side of a sphere or circle to the other, passing through the centre.

Does Pluto have a moon?
Pluto has one moon that orbits it. The moon's name is Charon. Charon is half the size of Pluto.

What is Pluto like?
Pluto is dark and cold. It is too far away from the Sun to receive much light or heat.

This white streak of stars is called the Milky Way.

Early astronomy

In ancient times, people did not understand the objects in the night sky. Every night, thousands of stars seemed to move across the sky. People did not know that stars are balls of very hot gases that give off heat and light. They did not know that the Earth spins. Today, people know that it is the Earth's spin that makes the stars seem to move.

Astronomers are scientists who study objects in space. Early astronomers carefully studied stars in the sky. They watched five special objects in the night sky. These objects stood out because they were in different places in the sky every night. They did not follow the same path as the rest of the objects in the sky.

Names

Early **astronomers** named each of the five strange moving objects after gods and goddesses in Roman myths. A myth is a story which trys to explain things in nature.

They named one object Mercury, the messenger god. Another object they named Venus, after the goddess of love and beauty in Roman myths. The three other objects were named Mars, Jupiter and Saturn. Mars was the Roman god of war, Jupiter was the god of the sky and Saturn was the god of agriculture.

Today, **astronomers** know that those five objects are planets. A planet is a large spherical object that travels around a star. Planets do not give off light. Instead, they reflect light from the star they **orbit**.

The Sun is a star. The planets travel around the Sun in paths called orbits. Nine planets that orbit the Sun have been identified in our **solar system**.

The planet closest to the Sun is Mercury. The next closest planet is Venus. Further away is the Earth, then Mars, Jupiter, Saturn, Uranus, Neptune and, last of all, Pluto. A tenth planet-like object was found orbiting the Sun in June 2002, but at just half the size of Pluto, scientists are not sure that it can actually be called a planet.

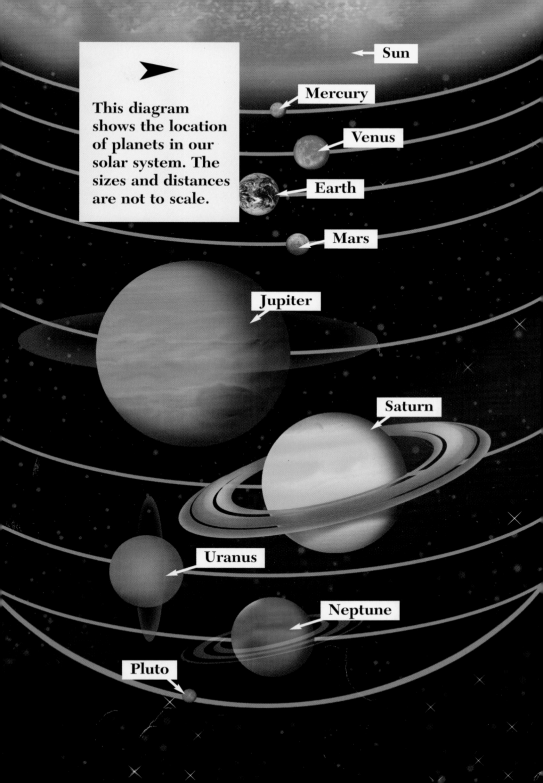

Sun

Mercury

Venus

This diagram shows the location of planets in our solar system. The sizes and distances are not to scale.

Earth

Mars

Jupiter

Saturn

Uranus

Neptune

Pluto

The Sun's high density gives it the greatest gravitational pull in the solar system.

Gravity and the Sun

The Sun is the **solar system**'s largest and densest object. Density is the amount of material squeezed into a certain space. The denser an object is, the more it pulls on objects around it. This pull is an object's **gravity**. Gravity is a natural force that attracts objects to each other.

The Sun has a stronger gravitational pull than any other object in our solar system. The closer a planet is to the Sun, the more the Sun's gravitational force affects it.

Early beliefs

Early **astronomers** believed the night sky was a great black shell surrounding the Earth. They thought that the stars were lights on the shell. They also thought that the Sun and the Moon were on the shell.

Those early astronomers believed the shell spun around the Earth. They thought that the stars moved because the shell was spinning. Astronomers thought planets were on their own shells because the planets did not move in the same way as the stars.

Until the 1700s, astronomers knew of only five planets other than the Earth. These were the close planets Mercury, Venus, Mars, Jupiter and Saturn. They were very bright and easy to see. Astronomers did not know about the three planets furthest away from the Earth. These planets are too dim to be seen without telescopes.

Discovery of Uranus

Astronomers needed a new tool to see dim, faraway objects. They needed a tool that made distant objects appear bigger and brighter. The tool they invented was the telescope.

Scientists Hans Lippershey and Galileo Galilei made the first telescopes in 1608 and 1609. Galileo made many discoveries about stars with his telescope. He studied a white streak in the night sky called the Milky Way. He learned that the white streak was the combined light of many stars.

Sir William Herschel also made telescopes. In 1781, he was looking through one of the telescopes he had built. He aimed the telescope at a group of stars.

Among the stars, Herschel spotted a blue-green dot. Watching the path of the dot over several nights, he realized that it moved like a planet and not like a star. Herschel's blue dot was another planet.

Herschel named the new planet Georgium Sidus, which means Star of George. The name was in honour of his patron, King George III. A patron is somebody who gives money so a person can work on special projects.

The name of Herschel's planet changed twice. For a time, it was called Herschel in honour of its discoverer. In the early 1800s, the name Uranus was suggested by astronomer Johann Elert Bode. In Greek myths, Uranus is the god of the heavens. By the late 1800s, Herschel's planet became known to everyone as Uranus.

Astronomers used mathematics to find the eighth planet, Neptune.

Telescopes and planet hunting

Astronomers now knew of seven planets in the solar system. Some wondered if there might be more planets beyond Uranus. The telescopes the astronomers used were not strong enough to see any other planets. Planet hunting with telescopes can be difficult. Only nearby planets can be seen easily.

Telescopes use lenses and mirrors to collect light. To collect light from faraway objects, lenses and mirrors must be large. The larger the lenses and mirrors are, the more light they collect.

In fact, telescopes collect too much light for astronomers to see planets outside the solar system. The brightness of distant stars covers up any planets that might circle them. Astronomers cannot see these planets with a telescope. To make their next discoveries, astronomers turned to mathematics.

Discovering Neptune

In early 1846, astronomers watched Uranus moving oddly in its **orbit**. They had been studying Uranus and had mapped what they thought was its normal movement. But sometimes Uranus moved faster or slower than astronomers expected.

Some astronomers thought another planet was changing Uranus's orbit. They thought this new planet's **gravity** was the force making Uranus go faster or slower than expected. Using mathematics, astronomer Urbain Jean Joseph LeVerrier predicted where the new planet would be. Later in 1846, Johann Gottfried Galle aimed a telescope at LeVerrier's predicted location. He found the eighth planet. The new planet was named Neptune. Neptune is further away and fainter than Uranus. It is nearly 4500 million kilometres (2800 million miles) from the Sun.

This is an artist's drawing of what the planet Pluto looks like.

Pluto, the ninth planet

Neptune's movements puzzled **astronomers**. They decided that there must be another planet **orbiting** the Sun. They felt that this planet's **gravitational** force was pulling on Neptune and causing it to move oddly. Some astronomers nicknamed the mystery planet 'Planet X'.

In the early 1900s, Percival Lowell was one of the astronomers who believed that there was a Planet X. Lowell had an observatory in Arizona, in the USA. An observatory is a building with a large telescope inside it. Lowell's observatory sat on a high hill where the night sky was very dark. It was the perfect place to use a telescope.

Lowell searched for Planet X for eleven years.
He died before the planet was discovered.

Search for Planet X

In 1905, Lowell decided to look for Planet X. Lowell searched for the mysterious planet secretly. He did not want other **astronomers** to know what he was doing. If they did, Lowell was afraid they might make the discovery first.

Lowell began taking photographs of the night sky. A few days later, he took another photograph of the same section of sky. Lowell looked at the photographs with a magnifying glass. He looked for any star that seemed to move. If he found such a star, he knew it would not be a star at all. It would be Planet X.

Lowell worked hard and his health suffered. In 1912, he collapsed. He later recovered, but he knew he needed to find a better way to look for Planet X.

The new tool Lowell found was called a blink comparator. The blink comparator projected pictures on a screen. The pictures flashed back and forth. First, Lowell would see one picture of the sky. Then he would see the second picture of the sky. This made it easier to see if an object had moved.

Even with the blink comparator, Lowell never found Planet X. He died in 1916, fourteen years before Planet X was discovered.

This is a photograph of the pictures Tombaugh used to discover Pluto.

Clyde Tombaugh

Clyde Tombaugh grew up on a farm. He loved **astronomy** and built his own telescopes using parts from his father's machines. He looked at Mars and Jupiter and sketched what he saw.

In 1928, Tombaugh sent his sketches to the Lowell Observatory. Astronomers at the observatory liked Tombaugh's pictures. They asked Tombaugh to come to the observatory to work. Tombaugh arrived there in 1929.

At the Lowell Observatory, Tombaugh's only job was to search for Planet X. For months he used a telescope to take pictures of the night sky. After waiting several days, he took more pictures of the same places.

Like Lowell, Tombaugh used a blink comparator to look at both pictures. Tombaugh looked for objects that changed position between the time the two pictures were taken.

Not many visiting astronomers took Tombaugh's search seriously. They laughed at Tombaugh when they visited the Lowell Observatory. They did not think that he would find anything with his improved blink comparator. They did not think it was possible to find another planet. They thought the planet would be too far away to see.

On 18 February 1930, Tombaugh proved them wrong. He compared two pictures with the blink comparator. He noticed that a tiny dot had moved. The tiny dot looked just like any other star. Tombaugh saw millions of dim stars just like it, but stars do not move. Tombaugh had found Planet X.

Pluto is so far away that it looks fuzzy in pictures taken by telescopes.

Naming Planet X

Naming the new planet was almost as hard as finding it. Many different people and newspapers suggested names for Planet X. Lowell's wife first wanted the new planet to be named after her husband. Then she wanted it to be named Constance, after herself. One **astronomer** at the observatory wanted to name the new planet Minerva. In Roman myths, Minerva is the goddess of wisdom.

An eleven-year-old English schoolgirl called Venetia Burney suggested the name Pluto for the planet.

In Roman myths, Pluto was god of the underworld. The underworld is where people went after they died. People felt that the name suited the planet. Pluto is so far away that it is dark and cold like the mythological underworld. Also, the first two letters of Pluto are P and L. These were Percival Lowell's initials. Pluto turned out to be the perfect name.

Studying Pluto

After Tombaugh's discovery, astronomers began studying Pluto. But Pluto is so far away that it is very hard to see and study. Not much sunlight reaches Pluto, and even less reflects back. Even the most powerful telescopes cannot make Pluto clear enough for astronomers to see it well.

Pluto is the smallest known planet in the **solar system**. It is only 2300 kilometres (1400 miles) in diameter. The Earth is more than five times larger than Pluto. The Earth's diameter is about 12,756 kilometres (7926 miles). Pluto would fit inside the borders of the USA.

> **This is an artist's drawing of Pluto and its moon, Charon, orbiting the Sun.**

Pluto's orbit

Pluto **orbits** the Sun at an average distance of about 5900 million kilometres (3700 million miles). It takes Pluto 248 Earth years to travel once around the Sun. Because it is so far away from the Sun, Pluto is a cold planet. Its average temperature is –220°C (–428°F).

Astronomers have studied Pluto's orbit. They have learned that its orbit is unlike the orbits of the other planets in our **solar system**. The orbits of the other eight planets are almost perfect circles, but Pluto's orbit is elliptical. Elliptical means shaped like a stretched-out circle.

Until they studied Pluto's orbit, astronomers had thought that the solar system was nearly flat. But Pluto's orbit is tilted about 17° from the other planets' orbits.

Because of its elliptical orbit, Pluto is not always the same distance away from the Sun. During one part of its orbit, it is about 7400 million kilometres (4600 million miles) from the Sun. During another part of its orbit, it is only about 4300 million kilometres (2700 million miles) from the Sun.

Along part of Pluto's orbit, it is closer to the Sun than Neptune is. During that time, Neptune is the most distant planet from the Sun. This part of Pluto's orbit lasts 20 years. It last happened from February 1979 to February 1999. It will not happen again until the year 2228.

This is the clearest view of Pluto's surface. It was taken by a space telescope.

Pluto's surface

Astronomers have many questions about Pluto. They want to know what its surface is like. They want to know if it has an **atmosphere**. An atmosphere is a layer of gases that surrounds an object in space. No space probe has ever flown near Pluto. A space probe is a craft built to explore and gather information about space.

The Hubble Space Telescope took the best pictures of Pluto. The Hubble is a powerful telescope on a spacecraft that **orbits** the Earth. The Hubble's pictures show light and dark patches on Pluto's surface. From these pictures, astronomers can see that Pluto looks something like Neptune's moon Triton.

Triton is the largest of Neptune's moons. It can be seen from the Earth. In 1989, astronomers learned a lot about Triton when the *Voyager 2* space probe flew by and took pictures of it. The surface of Triton is made from rock and ice.

Astronomers think that Pluto is also made of rock, ice and frozen gases, mainly nitrogen. The atmosphere remains frozen because Pluto is so far from the Sun for most of its orbit. **Craters** and other features on its surface may cause Pluto's patches. They may also be caused by frost that moves across Pluto's surface as the seasons change.

Astronomers are still not sure what causes the light and dark patches on Pluto. One of the first tasks of a space probe visiting Pluto will be to find out. NASA is planning a mission called *New Horizons,* which will explore Pluto and the region of the solar system beyond it. This area is full of small icy orbiting objects, and is called the **Kuiper Belt**.

Charon

For many years, **astronomers** thought Pluto had no moons. But in 1978, astronomer James Christy was looking at pictures of Pluto. The pictures were not very clear, but Christy noticed something strange. Pluto seemed to have a bump on it.

Christy looked at other pictures of Pluto. He saw the bump again, but the bump was in different places. Christy realized that it was not a bump at all. It was a moon **orbiting** Pluto.

Christy named Pluto's moon Charon. In Greek myths, Charon was a boatman who took the souls of the dead across the River Styx to the underworld. But Christy had a different reason for calling the moon Charon. He was naming it in honour of his wife, Charlene.

Charon is probably made of frozen water and nitrogen. It orbits at an average distance of about 19,600 kilometres (12,180 miles) from Pluto. Charon is a small moon, only 1250 kilometres (780 miles) in diameter. It is almost half the size of Pluto. Some astronomers call Pluto and Charon a double planet because they are so close in size.

Charon is one of the few moons in the **solar system** with an **atmosphere**. Astronomers think that this atmosphere is really Pluto's. They think that Charon is so close to Pluto that Charon orbits within Pluto's atmosphere.

Astronomers have learned the most about Charon from pictures taken by the Hubble Space Telescope. The pictures show that Charon's colour is different from Pluto's. Astronomers study the different colours to figure out what the planet and its moon are made from. They think Pluto's surface is rock and solid **methane** and its atmosphere is rich in methane gas. They think that the surface of Charon is ice.

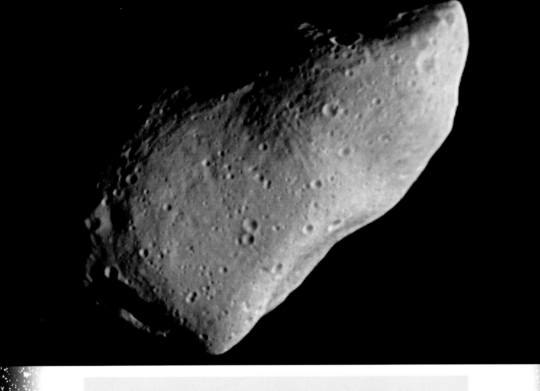

▲ **Some people think Pluto is an asteroid like this one. This asteroid is named Gaspra.**

The minor planet

Many **astronomers** believe that Pluto is not actually a planet for several reasons. Firstly, it is the only planet made of rock and frozen gases. Secondly, it is so much smaller than the other planets. Thirdly, the shape of its **orbit** is different from all the other planets.

Some astronomers think that Pluto is really an asteroid. An asteroid is a large, irregularly shaped rock in space. Most asteroids are only a few kilometres in diameter. The largest known asteroid is Ceres. It is around 950 kilometres (590 miles) in diameter. Most asteroids in the **solar system** orbit the Sun in the asteroid belt. This is an area between Mars and Jupiter, full of thousands of asteroids.

Astronomers who say Pluto is a planet point out that asteroids are irregularly shaped, but Pluto is spherical like a planet. They also point out that asteroids are not large enough to have an **atmosphere**. They think that Pluto has an atmosphere, like a planet.

Other astronomers think Pluto is really a comet. A comet is a large ball of ice, dust and rock. Many comets travel in orbits that bring them close to the Sun. The Sun's heat melts some of the ice. Gases stream off and form a tail. Some astronomers think Pluto's frozen surface might form a tail if it passed near the sun. But Pluto is much larger than any known comet.

Still other astronomers say that Pluto is a different kind of planet. They say that it is a minor planet, and the rest of the planets are major planets. Astronomers are now searching the area of space beyond Pluto, the **Kuiper Belt**, for more minor planets. The recent discovery in this region of an object similar to Pluto has weakened the argument that Pluto is a true planet.

Clyde Tombaugh discovered Pluto by chance. The measurements he used were wrong.

Planet hunting

When Clyde Tombaugh looked for Pluto, he used Percival Lowell's measurements of Neptune's **orbit** to aim his telescope. Other **astronomers** checked these measurements. They also looked closely at Pluto's **gravitational** pull. They found that Neptune is more than 8000 times bigger than Pluto. That means Pluto is much too small to have an effect on Neptune. Astronomers found that the measurements Tombaugh used were actually wrong. He had discovered Pluto by chance.

Astronomers had a new problem. Something unknown was causing the changes in Neptune's orbit. Astronomers began looking for another Planet X.

If there is another Planet X, astronomers think it is even futher away than Pluto. It might be the same size as Pluto. If so, it would be very difficult to find.

Planet hunting with space probes

Scientists want to get closer to planets than they can with telescopes. That is why they send space probes out into the **solar system**. The space probes send back information that helps the scientists learn.

Scientists use a planet's **gravity** to help steer the space probes. When a probe comes close to a planet, the planet's gravity pulls on it. This speeds up the probe. It also pulls the probe into a path that curves around the planet. Scientists use this curving to change a space probe's path. This way, the space probe can visit other planets.

In 1972 and 1973, scientists launched the *Pioneer 10* and *Pioneer 11* space probes. These probes passed through the asteroid belt and flew near Jupiter in December 1973 and December 1974. *Pioneer 10* then continued on its way out of the solar system. It was the first space probe sent beyond the solar system, but it will take 2 million years to reach the nearest star in its path. *Pioneer 11* flew past Saturn in September 1979.

In 1977, scientists launched the *Voyager 1* and *Voyager 2* space probes. These probes flew near Jupiter in 1979, taking pictures and measurements. Jupiter's gravity redirected the probes out into space.

Pioneer 11

Voyager 2

Pioneer 10

▲ **This diagram shows the paths the different space probes travelled.**

Each of the *Pioneer* and *Voyager* probes is heading in a different direction.

Scientists are tracking the journeys of these space probes. They are hoping that one will pass near an unknown planet. Then the planet's gravity will change the space probe's path. This will help scientists know where to look for a new planet. But no space probe paths have been changed so far.

Pluto and Charon orbit each other.
This makes Pluto appear to wobble.

To see how this works, imagine two balls
connected by a stick. The balls are Pluto
and Charon. The stick represents gravity. The rope
is where Pluto and Charon are balanced.
When Pluto and Charon orbit, they twirl
around the balance point.

This diagram of Pluto and Charon shows
how wobbling happens.

Wobbling

It is possible that scientists have discovered all the planets **orbiting** the Sun. There might not be another Planet X, but **astronomers** are also looking for planets orbiting other stars.

To discover distant planets, astronomers use telescopes in a special way. They do not use them to look directly at planets. Instead, they look for star wobble. Star wobble occurs when a star moves one way and then the other. Star wobble is movement caused by a planet's **gravity**. If the wobble repeats, astronomers know that there is a planet orbiting the star.

Astronomers can learn many things by watching stars wobble. If a star wobbles a long way back and forth, the planet orbiting the star is very massive. If a star wobbles only a little back and forth, the planet orbiting the star is not very massive. If a star wobbles back and forth quickly, the planet is in a close orbit around the star. If a star wobbles back and forth slowly, the planet is in a distant orbit around the star.

Red shift

In 1995, **astronomers** began to discover new planets outside our **solar system**. They used the wobble method to find some of them. The first ones they found were very large. These produced big wobbles in their stars so they were the easiest to see.

Astronomers have found other planets by watching to see if a star's colour seems to change. Stars that are tugged by a planet's **gravitational** force seem to change colour only slightly. A star looks slightly more red if a planet's gravity pulls it away from the Earth. A star looks slightly more blue if a planet's gravity pulls it towards the Earth. This change in the appearance of the star's colour is known to astronomers as red shift.

Since 1995, astronomers have found more than 30 stars that have planets **orbiting** them. All of the new planets are large. Because they are so large, astronomers compare the new planets to the size of Jupiter. Jupiter is the largest planet in our solar system. It is more than 1300 times bigger than the Earth. Some of the newly discovered planets astronomers have found are only about half as big as Jupiter. Others are eleven times bigger.

Astronomers compare planets that orbit other stars to Jupiter.

Scientists study stars like this to find planets. They use the black area to block starlight so they can study it. This star has a disc of gas and dust around it. Planets might form here.

Upsilon Andromedae

Astronomers are getting better at finding new planets. With practise, they have begun to find smaller planets. Today, distant planets the size of Saturn and Uranus have been found.

Astronomers have found one star that has at least three large planets orbiting it. The star is called Upsilon Andromedae. Upsilon Andromedae is a sun-like star. It is about three times as bright as the Sun and can be seen by the naked eye. It is about 44 light years away from the Earth. A light year is the distance light travels in one Earth year. Astronomers use light years when measuring great distances.

Astronomers believe that Upsilon Andromedae's planet system is a lot like our **solar system**. In 1996, astronomers found one planet very close to Upsilon Andromedae. The closest planet to the Sun in our solar system is Mercury. The planet closest to Upsilon Andromedae is much closer than Mercury is to our Sun. It is about 70 per cent of the mass of Jupiter.

The second and third planets orbiting Upsilon Andromedae were discovered in 1999. The second planet is about as far out as the Earth is from the Sun. It is about twice the mass of Jupiter. The third planet orbiting Upsilon Andromedae is about three times further away from the star than the Earth is from the Sun. It is four times bigger than Jupiter.

Astronomers do not know if an Earth-sized planet is also orbiting Upsilon Andromedae. The **gravity** from such a planet would not be strong enough to change the movement or observed colour of Upsilon Andromedae. Astronomers would not be able to see any changes in the star through their telescopes.

This diagram compares the planets around Pulsar B1257+12 to our inner solar system.

Pulsar planets

Astronomers study many different kinds of stars in the night sky. One special kind of star is called a pulsar. Pulsars are the smallest stars. They are usually only about 16 kilometres (10 miles) across. All stars spin, but pulsars spin quickly because they are so small.

Each time a pulsar spins, it sends a wave of energy that travels to the Earth. The pulses of energy travel through space like lighthouse signals. Each pulsar has its own pulse rate. It may pulse once every four seconds or hundreds of times per second. Each pulsar always pulses at the same rate.

Since 1967, astronomers have discovered hundreds of pulsars. In 1992, astronomer Alexander Wolszczan studied the pulsar called PSR B1257+12. He noticed that its pulse changed. He knew that a pulsar's pulse should never change. Something else had to be changing PSR B1257+12's pulse. Wolszczan discovered that three very small planets were **orbiting** PSR B1257+12. The **gravity** from the planets was changing the rate of PSR B1257+12's pulse.

Some astronomers think PSR B1257+12's planets were created from an explosion. They think an exploding star sent dust and gas into space. Gravity pulled the dust and gas together into clumps. Smaller clumps joined together when they crashed into each other. They became larger clumps and continued to grow over millions of years until they became the planets that now orbit PSR B1257+12.

Scientists believe the Milky Way Galaxy looks like this spiral galaxy.

Protoplanets

Our **solar system** is part of the Milky Way Galaxy. A galaxy is a very large system of stars and objects **orbiting** stars. A galaxy is held together by **gravity**. There are millions of stars in the Milky Way. With so many stars, there are many chances for planets to form around them. **Astronomers** will probably continue to find new planets in the Milky Way and in other galaxies.

Astronomers looking for new planets often study nebulas. Nebulas are large clouds of gas and dust. Sometimes astronomers see small objects forming in the nebulas. They think these objects are new planets. Astronomers call these new planets **protoplanets**.

Astronomers are always coming up with new tools to help them do their work. They build more powerful telescopes. They have also planned new space probes to find planets.

One planned space probe is called the *Terrestrial Planet Finder*. Astronomers will use it to study planets and find new ones. Scientists hope to launch the *Terrestrial Planet Finder* sometime around 2012.

Another planned space probe is called the *Kepler Mission*. *Kepler* will study the changes in brightness of about 900,000 stars. Some planets may pass in front of the star they are orbiting. If they do, the star will get dimmer because the planet blocks some of the star's light. The *Kepler Mission* would detect this. Scientists hope to find several hundred Earth-sized planets in the habitable zone around Sun-like stars, where life might survive.

Astronomers will use these new tools and invent others. They will continue to find more planets and make new discoveries.

Glossary

astronomer scientist who studies objects in space

atmosphere layer of gases that surround a planet

crater bowl-shaped hole left when a meteorite strikes an object in space

gravity force that attracts all objects to each other; the gravitational force exerted by an object depends on its mass

Kuiper Belt (KI-per) swarm of objects made of ice and rock that orbit the Sun beyond Neptune

methane (MEE-thayn) gas made out of carbon and hydrogen

orbit path an object travels around another object in space

protoplanet newly forming planet

solar system all the objects that orbit around a star

Further information

Websites
BBC Science
http://www.bbc.co.uk/science/space/
British National Space Centre
http://www.bnsc.gov.uk/
European Space Agency
http://sci.esa.int/
**Star Child: A Learning Centre for
                Young Astronomers**
http://starchild.gsfc.nasa.gov/

Books
*Exploring the solar system: Uranus, Pluto and
    Neptune*, Giles Sparrow
    (Heinemann Library, 2001)
The Universe: The Outer Planets, Raman Prinja
    (Heinemann Library, 2002)

Useful address
London Planetarium
Marylebone Road, London
NW1 5LR

Index